Man's Diagnosis
God's Prognosis

Man's Diagnosis God's Prognosis

Standing Against a Killer, Melanoma

Don Davis

Pleasant Word (a division of WinePress Publishing, PO Box 428, Enumclaw, WA 98022) functions only as book publisher. As such, the ultimate design, content, editorial accuracy, and views expressed or implied in this work are those of the author.

Unless otherwise noted, all Scriptures are taken from the *King James Version* of the Bible.

All hymn quotations are from the *Baptist Hymnal*®, Copyright 1975 Convention Press. These quotes come from hymns that are at least 50 years old and are in the public domain.

ISBN 13: 978-1-4141-1663-1
ISBN 10: 1-4141-1663-2
Library of Congress Catalog Card Number: 2010900305

Contents

Acknowledgments. vii

1. The Driving Force. 1
2. In the Beginning, God. 5
3. Back Where We Started. 13
4. When We Least Expect It 23
5. Another Miracle Coming Up. 29
6. Letting God Fight the Daily Battles. 35
7. Helping Others Along the Way. 41
8. A Major Setback 47
9. A Double Dose of Recovery. 53
10. Recognizing a Victory. 57
11. Post Treatment:
        Almost Twelve Years Later 59

12. An Ounce of Prevention 65

13. What Does the Future Bring? 73

14. The Real Survivors 75

Acknowledgments

SO MANY PEOPLE were involved with my melanoma treatment and recovery that I could not possibly recognize them all. Therefore, I have selected the three people who played the most significant part.

First, I must thank my dear wife, Barbara, for all the loving support and encouragement she provided to me. She was by my side day in and day out, holding my hand and saying, "We are going to make it because God has more for us to do in fulfilling His will for our lives. God will give us the victory, for He is much greater than any type of disease." Although at times the road to recovery seemed far off, she never once doubted that God was in control and that we would be the victors.

Second, I could not begin to show enough appreciation to Dr. Barry Leshin at the Skin Surgery Center in Winston Salem, North Carolina. Dr. Leshin is the best doctor I have ever met. Anyone who has ever been treated by Dr. Leshin would not only attest to his expertise in the field of dermatology but also in his ability to be a people's doctor with compassion like none other I have ever seen. My testimony is that without his care and professional knowledge of melanoma, I probably would not be alive today. I have been seeing Dr. Leshin for more than sixteen years, and not once did I visit his office and not get the impression that I was his most important patient. I am sure he treats everyone the same.

Last, but certainly not least, I have to commend my oncologist, Dr. Paul Savage of the Wake Forest Physicians Baptist Medical Center in Winston Salem, North Carolina, for giving me the best treatment a person could receive. Dr. Savage knew what I needed and set out with the goal to provide the necessary treatment to save my life. He has always been honest in answering my questions and providing me with the good news and the bad. Dr. Savage is a compassionate doctor.

The Driving Force

*And this I pray, that your love may abound
yet more and more in knowledge and
in all judgment.*
—Philippians 1:9

EARLY IN MY experience with melanoma, I was determined to write a book to help others who had to face a similar journey through this type of cancer. This goal had been fueled by the books I was able to read during the first stages of my treatment. The late Larry Burkett's book *Nothing to Fear: The Key to Cancer Survival* and Charles Swindoll's *Learning to Laugh Again* were especially helpful to me. When I finished reading these jewels I passed them to others, who also received encouragement from the writings.

I had often thought about how valuable it would be to have support-group testimonies readily available in written form so that people could receive ideas on how others were making it through their treatments. Cancer patients need to know that they are not the only ones feeling the way they are and that the symptoms from their cancer or the side effects from their medicines are not any different from others. Survivors need to do everything possible to help their fellow survivors through their fight with this awful disease. Of course, this book (or any others) will not replace attending a cancer support group because of the valuable information and personal fellowship a person can receive from those meetings.

Another incentive for me to get my story in print came from a statement made at a Blue Ridge Mountains Christian Writers Conference at the LifeWay Ridgecrest Christian Conference Center in Black Mountain, North Carolina. I had begun attending the conferences a few years earlier to receive tips on how to publish a book containing some of the articles I had written for a local newspaper. Without a doubt, the conference provides a full range of subjects that assist new writers in getting started in writing whatever type of book they desire.

That year during one of the breakout sessions, a lady asked the leader what he thought about writing a book concerning her daughter's fight with cancer. He replied, "There is no demand for books about people's cancer experiences unless the writer is a celebrity." What the lady thought about the session leader's response is unknown, but I was appalled that he would say such a thing. Of course, the young man was free to have such an opinion, and his answer could have been appropriate for someone who writes for financial gain, but it should not apply to those who write to help others along the way. Any writer would like to earn enough for his or her work to defray his or her expenses, and then some if possible. But how can God bless a Christian writer if money is his or her only goal?

Amazing as it may seem, later that evening during the combined conference meeting, the guest speaker somewhat discounted the notion of writing for financial gain. He said that most of us sitting there would probably never write a bestseller. "On the other hand," he said, "if God is leading you to write on a particular subject, sit down and write it. Your book may not be a bestseller, but God may have chosen you to write exactly what someone needs to read right now." I came away from that meeting knowing that I had to tell my story, which could help someone in his or her long journey through cancer recovery.

So now you know why this book has been written. As you read, please do not get alarmed if the medical jargon is not exactly as it should be or if some of the recommendations are not exactly as you would see them. Remember that my goal is to help—nothing that is being said here is intended to hinder or hurt anyone. As I say throughout the book, none of us know everything—we just know what we have experienced and hope that it will aid someone in their battle with cancer.

In the Beginning, God

*In the beginning God created the
heavens and the earth.*
—Genesis 1:1

IN EVERY STORY there is a beginning. In the Bible, Genesis 1:1 launches into the creation of the heavens and the earth and continues to the introduction of God to mankind. "In the beginning, God" is paramount to all other truths. His existence is what holds this world together. Mankind cannot exist without Him. He is sovereign—no one or anything can compare to Him, for He is God.

My story begins and ends with God, because it was through Him and by Him that I was able to overcome the terrible disease of melanoma, which is considered to be one of the worst cancers (if not the worst). In Jeremiah 1:5, the Lord spoke to the prophet Jeremiah, saying, "Before I formed thee in the belly I knew thee." God is omniscient. He knew when my ordeal with this dreadful disease would begin, and He also knew that He would give me the victory in overcoming this awful disease.

In 1993, having experienced a full life including more than twenty years of service in the United States Air Force, fifteen years in business, and a third career as pastor of Memorial Baptist Church, I was diagnosed with melanoma. I had noticed a small brown spot on my nose, but I had never given it much thought. My dermatologist had checked it several years previously and had removed some spots he called "precancerous cells" from my face. Like many people, I never thought I would get cancer, so I ignored scheduling follow-up examinations.

One Sunday morning after the worship service, a church member, Suzan Jarman, asked if I had noticed the brown spot on my nose. (She had evidently read about some of the symptoms of skin cancer.) I shrugged it off and said, "I will get it checked out." Although I was not greatly concerned, I conferred with my wife, Barbara, and we agreed that the best thing to do was for me to see a dermatologist.

Some would say that Suzan's watchful eye was by chance, but in hindsight, I know that it was divine appointment. The next week, I had an appointment with my ear, nose and throat (ENT) physician, Dr. Lynn Hughes, and decided to show him the spot, as he had previously performed skin cancer surgery on some of our church members. When he examined the spot, he indicated that it could be cancerous and suggested that I undergo a biopsy, which he did during that visit. The appointment was on a Friday, which delayed me getting the results until Monday.

As any cancer survivor can affirm, there is normally a waiting period between any type of test and the results. The agony builds with each delay, because the "not knowing" factor makes the pressure grow. I can't say I did not worry or think about the test results that weekend. Having read, preached and quoted 2 Timothy 1:7, which says, "For God hath not given us a spirit of fear; but of power, and of love and a sound mind," gave some comfort. However, now I was having to practice that promise, and I discovered that it was not easy to trust God completely.

Staying busy doing my final preparations for two Sunday messages and being in church on Sunday helped the situation. Also, being with God's people, sharing my problem and praying with them relieved some of the anxiety and left me with a peace that could not be explained. God gave me peace in the midst of a storm.

A call to the doctor's office on Monday revealed that the results had not come back. The tension continued to grow by leaps and bounds all that day. I spent another day and night searching for peace.

On Tuesday morning, Dr. Hughes's nurse called and relayed a message asking me to come to their office at 2 P.M. I spent that morning in prayer asking

God for peace and to let the time pass quickly. I knew that only He could give me what was needed. "Thou wilt keep him in perfect peace, whose mind is stayed on thee: because he trusted in thee" (Isa. 26:3). I knew that I could accept whatever the answer might be.

During the drive to the doctor's office, I listened to WMIT, a local Christian radio station in Black Mountain, North Carolina. An evangelist was telling about his cancer experience and how God had blessed him. Although this man did not know it, he was a messenger from God confirming to me the results of the biopsy and also that God would be with me and see me through. Sure enough, when I walked into the office, Dr. Hughes, with as much compassion as a Christian doctor could have, confirmed that the spot on my nose was melanoma and suggested surgery. No other choice seemed available but to remove the cancer from my body. His recommendation was to remove the diseased area from my nose and replace it with a graft of skin from behind my ear. I agreed to the procedure and set up an appointment for surgery.

I walked immediately over to Cabarrus Memorial Hospital (Now Carolinas Medical Center Northeast), where my wife worked. Not knowing how Barbara would react to the news, I asked her to step out into the hallway where we could talk privately. I did not hold back but immediately told her that the test was positive for melanoma. Obviously, she already knew because I could not keep the tears from flowing. As she began to cry, I held her in my arms while we prayed for God to give us strength for the bumpy road we had to face. We had no doubt that God was as near as always and that the melanoma would not defeat us. Even in the face of a major trial, we could say, "But thanks be to God, which gives us the victory through our Lord Jesus Christ" (1 Cor. 15:57).

The surgery had been scheduled a couple of weeks away. I cannot remember exactly the reason for the delay, but I recall that God provided a way for us to pass the time. My wife, Barbara, our son Steve, his wife, Leigh Ann, and our friends Brenda Overcash and Judy Rich had reservations for the Southern Baptist Convention in Houston, Texas. The 1,600-mile ride was uncomfortable for me, because I had gotten into some poison ivy while weed-eating my yard and I was constantly fighting not to scratch it. The poison ivy had spread over my arms and torso and was causing me great discomfort. Despite this, it was evident the Lord had planned this trip, for we never laughed so much in our lives. Laughter took my mind off the poison ivy and the impending surgery. In addition, being at the convention provided the spiritual lift I needed at that time. The Lord has told us to "rejoice and be exceedingly glad; for great is your reward in heaven" (Matt. 5:12a).

The surgery was performed in late June in Dr. Hughes's office. The cancerous area was removed and replaced with the graft as planned. The pain was not excessive, and I required little pain medication following the surgery. Although the fix had been accomplished and Dr. Hughes had done everything he had promised, an uneasy feeling settled in the bottom of my stomach. My question to God was, "Lord, are You speaking to me? Should I share what I'm feeling with someone else?"

The next week when Dr. Hughes removed the bandage, I didn't think the scar looked good. There was definitely an indention on my nose. The question now was whether the sunk-in area would leave me disfigured like some of the other people I had seen after having a similar type of surgery. When I inquired whether all the cancer had been removed, Dr. Hughes indicated that there could still be precancerous cells. When I shared my apprehensions with Barbara and our children, Donald, Gail and Steven, they too had doubts. For more than two weeks, the questions continued. After much prayer and asking God for direction, the consensus was that we needed a second opinion from a dermatologist. God's Word has told us, "If any of you lack wisdom, let him ask God, that gives to all men liberally, and upbraided not; and it shall be given him" (Jas. 1:5).

So we made an appointment with Dr. John Hoover. At the time of the examination, I told the doctor of the biopsy report, which included the mention of precancerous cells. Dr. Hoover was not happy with this and called Dr. Hughes. Since the prognosis was not clear, we decided on a third opinion. That same day, we made an appointment with Dr. Barry Leshin, a dermatologist who was a melanoma skin cancer specialist at Baptist Hospital in Winston Salem, North Carolina. Dr. Hoover referred to Dr. Leshin as "the best in the business." He had such a high opinion of Dr. Leshin because he had studied under him at Wake Forest School of Medicine.

This information gave my family and me confidence that Dr. Leshin was the right doctor to see. We scheduled the appointment for mid-July. We needed answers, and God was providing them. "Beloved, if our hearts condemn us not, then have we confidence toward God" (1 John 3:21).

Back Where We Started

Blessed are the poor in spirit:
for theirs is the kingdom of heaven.
—Matthew 5:3

THIS NEXT STEP was much like going back to the starting gate, but it provided me the peace I did not have up to that point. My spirit might not have been the best during every moment of every day, but God's hand was upon us, and I sensed His Spirit in my life. God's Spirit can surely give us comfort, as Ezekiel 36:27 states: "And I will put my Spirit within you, and cause you to walk in my statutes, and ye shall keep my judgments, and do them."

From day one, I felt comfortable with Dr. Leshin. He and his staff treated us with love and kindness, and immediately we could sense that they genuinely cared. The appointment with Dr. Leshin went well, and he laid out the game plan for me to return for surgery, where he would remove the graft and surrounding area until the biopsy showed negative for cancer cells. Plastic surgery would have to follow, but Dr. Leshin said we had to take one step at a time. The nurses warned us that on the day of the surgery we would have to stay overnight in the area because melanoma biopsies required at least twenty-four hours for the results to come back. I don't remember how long we had to wait to schedule the appointment for the surgery, but any delay would have been too long for me. I would have preferred to have the surgery performed that day just to get it over with.

Barbara and I returned home and informed our children about what was going to happen. Everyone agreed that we should proceed with the plan. Unfortunately, we discovered that the surgery had been scheduled during the same week our family had planned to spend some time together at Topsail Island Beach at the North Carolina coast. Since the beach cottage had already been rented and prepaid, Barbara and I convinced the children to continue with the plans. Of course, they were apprehensive about being away that week. We assured them that everything would be okay, as the surgery was to be performed as an outpatient procedure and we would be able to keep them informed of everything that was happening by phone.

To our advantage, our oldest son, Donald, lived in Kernersville, North Carolina, which was about thirty minutes from the hospital. We could stay at his home overnight if more surgery was needed the following day.

As I recall, the surgery took place on a Monday. The kids reluctantly left for Topsail Island on Saturday. I preached on Sunday, and after the service the congregation gathered around me at the altar for prayer. Just hearing people lift my name to God asking Him for mercy, kindness and healing provided the comfort I needed. We prayed for healing, just as the Bible tells us: "Is anyone sick among you? Let him call for the elders of the church; and let them pray over him, anointing him with oil in the name of the Lord" (Jas. 5:14). We did not use oil, but I knew God's Spirit had anointed me for surgery.

On Monday morning, Barbara and I drove to Winston Salem. God overwhelmed us with His presence and knowledge that everything would be okay. Barbara prayed for me before I was taken in to surgery. I could feel God's presence and felt a gentle touch all over, as if He were saying, "The LORD bless thee, and keep thee: The LORD make His face shine upon thee, and be gracious unto thee: The LORD lift up His countenance upon thee, and give thee peace" (Num. 6:24-26). Almost immediately after this, the assisting nurse came to get me and escorted me to the operating room.

Dr. Leshin injected my nose with medicine to numb the area where he would be operating. Without a doubt, the nose is one of the most sensitive places on the body. Tears ran down my face, but I knew that with the pain I was experiencing, not even the strongest person would have been able to hold back the tears. As the nurse prepped my face, she told me how good Dr. Leshin was and that there was no one better. She went on to tell me how compassionate he was with his patients. She indicated that Dr. Leshin was not in his profession for the money. He loved people. I told her about how the Great Physician was also present and that He too loved people.

God had surely sent me to the right doctor. Dr. Leshin was a doctor who cared about his patients, and at that moment a loving touch was certainly needed. Dr. Leshin completed the surgery in a short time. I did not know what I looked like or even remember having much pain, but I was glad that it was over. We left his office and returned to my son's home in Kernersville with instructions to call back the following morning to see if more surgery was needed.

Barbara and I spent the day and night waiting and praying that we would not have to go through another round of surgery. The next morning, we had breakfast and prayed again. Barbara called Dr. Leshin's office and was told that the report showed no evidence of cancer. Thus, no further surgery was necessary. We praised the Lord with all our hearts and souls. We felt like singing, "Worthy is the Lamb that was slain to receive power, and riches, and wisdom, and strength, and honor, and glory, and blessing" (Rev. 5:12b).

We did not have to return to the hospital that day, but the nurse gave Barbara a date and time for us to return so that Dr. Leshin could inspect the wound. The wound would have to heal before we could proceed with the plastic surgery. In the meantime, Dr. Leshin wanted us to meet with Dr. Malcolm W. Marks, who would do the plastic surgery in reconstructing the surface of my nose.

The bandage stayed on for a week, but then it had to be removed for healing to begin. I was self-conscious of my looks, but that was just the tip of the iceberg, considering what was to come. The people at Memorial Baptist Church were very understanding and allowed me to continue preaching on Sunday mornings even though the appearance of my nose was somewhat gruesome.

I don't recollect how long it took for my nose to heal from the surgery, but during that time we met with Dr. Marks. He explained the type of plastic surgery I was to receive, which was called a "Kazanjian forehead flap." His task was to remove a strip of skin from my forehead and attach it to the open scar on my nose. The flap from the forehead would remain on my nose until the nerves and blood circulated properly and it became attached. After three weeks, he would remove the flap from the graft and my forehead and the incision on my forehead would be closed. When I remarked about how far new technology had come, Dr. Marks informed me that the procedure had first been done in India more than 200 years ago.

Barbara and I left Dr. Marks's office somewhat confused about the details, but we trusted God and the doctor that everything would be okay. We would have to wait for another two weeks before the surgery could be performed. We had to remember that God's Word says, "But they that wait upon the Lord shall renew their strength; they shall mount up with wings of eagles; they shall run, and not be weary; and they shall walk, and not faint" (Isa. 40:31).

Finally, the day of the plastic surgery arrived. The procedure was to be done at the North Carolina Baptist Hospital surgical center. Barbara and our son Steve, an ordained minister, accompanied us for the early morning surgery. We had to be at the hospital at 5 A.M. for a 7 A.M. surgery. I distinctly remember Steve praying for me. Although there were still many unknowns, our spirits were high and we trusted that God would direct Dr. Marks's mind and hands through the surgery. Our faith was strong, and in our hearts we were agreeing with what the apostle Paul said: "For the which cause I also suffer these things: nevertheless I am not ashamed; for I know whom I have believed, and am persuaded that He is able to keep that which I have committed unto Him against that day" (2 Tim. 1:12).

The anesthesiologist in pre-op started the IV, and then I was wheeled back to the surgical holding area. Once there, I was informed that there would be a delay because of an unscheduled child's surgery, which had priority over all other surgeries. The wait was longer than expected, and the operating room nurses didn't come for me until about 9 A.M. Unfortunately, this information was not passed on to my family, and they began to worry when the surgery was not completed by 10 A.M. The news finally got to them, and they were much relieved.

I cannot remember exactly how long the surgery took, but I do remember the nurse in the recovery room saying, "Reverend Davis, are you okay?" My family met me in the room, where I would stay overnight. At that time my daughter Gail and my oldest son, Donald, had joined Barbara and Steve. What a joy to have all of them present to support their daddy. The bandage seemed to cover my entire face. As with most patients after surgery, hunger had set in. The nurses brought me a ham and cheese sandwich, which tasted like a delicious steak.

Our children went home in the early evening, but Barbara stayed with me through the night. Neither of us got much sleep, because every time I had to go to the bathroom, Barbara had to assist me with the IV pole. The next morning, Dr. Marks came to check my wounds and the bandage. He seemed to be very pleased and gave permission for me to go home later that morning. The discharge seemed to take forever, because Barbara had to be instructed in the care of the wound.

Steven had returned to Winston Salem to drive us home. The hour-and-a-half drive home seemed like an eternity. I had been on the fluid drip for more than twenty-four hours, and it had caused me to have to go to the restroom often. We did not even make it through the first town, Lexington, before we had to stop. The owner of the country store where we stopped seemed to feel sorry for me when he saw the big yellow bandage over my nose. I probably looked as if I had been badly beaten in a fight.

After stopping for lunch, we finally got home, where my number one "caregiver," Barbara, started her duties. The only thing I remember was sleeping most of the afternoon until she called me for dinner. The words of that old song, "His Eye is on the Sparrow," were very appropriate to us during that time. God was surely taking care of both of us, and I know that He was watching me.

The next morning, Barbara's big task was to remove the bandage and to care for the wound and the flap. She did a great job caring for me. Not many days had passed before we had to return to Dr. Marks for him to check the flap. The Lord spared me most of the pain throughout the recovery process.

The most embarrassing part of my ordeal was going to church with the bandages covering most of my face. I was not sure how the children would react. After preaching on the second Sunday, several children—Megan Sheets, Amanda Godfrey and Kaila Nicholson—came and hugged me and said they loved me. Sometimes adults back off when they see a hideous sight, but not children. God knew what I needed at the moment and sent it through the children.

That same weekend, another blessing awaited me. My two grandchildren, Brittany, who was five at the time, and Josh, who was a little over one year old, came to visit me. They completely overlooked the terrible-looking bandage on my face and did not back off from their granddaddy. The Bible says, "Lo, children are an heritage of the LORD: and the fruit of the womb is his reward" (Ps. 127:3). I have always interpreted this verse to mean that children are a blessing, which most of us will certainly agree. There were tears in my eyes, because my little ones accepted their granddaddy unconditionally.

After about two weeks, Barbara and I returned to the North Carolina Baptist Hospital, where the anesthetist put me to sleep and Dr. Marks removed the flap by snipping it at the forehead and graft sites. The pain was minimal again—evidently, my pain tolerance is quite high. For the next four to five months, I had to take cortisone injections to make the graft area on my nose rise to the original shape.

Barbara and I traveled to North Carolina Baptist Hospital on a weekly basis for the remainder of the year and into 1994. After this, we made monthly trips to the hospital until my nose began to take shape and the blood started circulating properly through the new graft. Each time Dr. Marks injected my nose, he would say, "Now comes the bee sting." To me, the pain was more excruciating than any bee sting I had ever experienced. Saying the Lord's Prayer provided a means of relieving the pain. When we cannot take it any longer, Jesus takes the overload on Himself.

To my joy, in February 1994 the last injection came, and I only had a few more appointments for Dr. Marks to check on his "work of art." He took photos of my nose throughout the stages of healing from start to finish. The surgery was truly a miracle, because most people today cannot tell that I have had surgery unless I tell them. Another noteworthy fact is that I preached most of the Sundays during the recovery process. I was able to completely fulfill my ministerial responsibilities at Memorial Baptist Church.

When We Least Expect It

*Trust in the LORD with all thine heart; and
lean not unto thine own understanding.
In all thy ways acknowledge Him,
and He shall direct thy paths.*
—Proverbs 3:5-6

THE REMAINDER OF 1994 was spent in follow-up visits to Dr. Leshin and Dr. Marks. During this time, we could see the miracle of surgery and God's provision in how my nose began to look normal again. Only one little spot of white was left on the tip, and that only appeared when my nose was cold. We could not stop praising the Lord. The time was appropriate to sing, "Praise Him, Praise Him, all ye little children, God is love, God is love."

The work at the church continued, and God blessed our family as well as the congregation. Except for chronic sinusitis, my body, energy and spiritual level were on the road to recovery. Only through God had I made it this far. As the apostle Paul wrote to young Timothy, "I exhort therefore, that, first of all, supplications, prayers, intercessions, and giving thanks, be made for all men; for kings, and for all that in authority; that we may lead a quiet and peaceable life in all godliness and honesty" (1 Tim. 2:1-2).

Then a tragedy hit Barbara and me. Her dad, Curtis Butler, became ill early in 1994, and she had to care for him as well as keep an eye on me. She did all this while still working. My wife was a real trooper who stood tall day in and day out despite knowing that her dad was getting worse and that he might not last much longer. He died on June 21, 1994. Later that same year, I was back at North Carolina Baptist Hospital for an outpatient hernia operation. I don't think anyone has ever had that type of surgery with less pain and fewer complications.

A highlight of 1995 was that in February my son Steve and I had the opportunity to travel to India on a mission trip. Considering my previous medical problems, I never dreamed of being able to travel in the states, much less go overseas. Nonetheless, God took care of me and allowed me to spend long days and into the night traveling to remote locations so that I could preach to hundreds of people who were hearing the gospel for the first time.

Later that year, my chronic sinusitis flared up, and Dr. Brian Matthews at Baptist Hospital in Winston Salem, North Carolina, had to perform surgery on my sinuses. I had to stay overnight in the hospital for the procedure. My spirits might have been dampened a little with this setback, but I knew that God was still with me and that He was carrying me all the way.

In early 1996, Dr. Matthews again operated on my sinuses to remove some blockages. As always, the presence of the Lord was in my midst, and again I was spared having severe pain or discomfort. David wrote, "He shall cover thee with his feathers, and under his wings shalt thou trust: his truth shall be thy shield and buckler" (Ps. 91:4).

In November 1996, my son Steve and I returned to India for a second time. The trip was a complete success, and my spirits were high. Then one morning while shaving, I discovered a small nodule just below my right ear. Because of my past history with melanoma, I knew that I could not ignore the bump—not taking it seriously could prove to be a deadly mistake.

Upon retuning home I told Barbara about the nodule, and we continued to monitor it through Christmas and even into 1997. In February the spot was still there, so I called Dr. Leshin's office to schedule an appointment. He let me come the next day. Since Barbara was working, I asked Steve to accompany me. At first Barbara was hesitant about this, but she finally agreed.

Steve and I drove up for an afternoon appointment with Dr. Leshin. He examined the spot but wasn't sure if the bump was cancerous, so he suggested that we do a biopsy of the node. Instead of having me go to the hospital lab, Dr. Leshin had a team come up and do the biopsy in his office. The procedure was painless and quick, and the technicians returned to the lab to determine if the growth was malignant. In a short time they called and reported that the node was positive for melanoma. The news was devastating. I had been clean for almost three years, but now the disease was back again. I can't describe the disappointment I felt at that moment.

Once more, Dr. Leshin handled the situation with the highest level of professionalism and compassion. He immediately offered encouragement, saying, "You have defeated the disease this far, and you can continue to keep up the fight." He soon came up with a plan to start treatment that would involve more surgery and probably some type of chemotherapy. Dr. Leshin had his administrative staff set up an appointment with Dr. Brian Logi, one of the best melanoma surgeons in America. In the meantime, he and the surgeon would decide the best course of action to take from there. Dr. Leshin also made an appointment with Dr. Paul Savage, an oncologist, who would prescribe other treatments following the surgery. Though the road ahead was not clear, I left Dr. Leshin's office feeling hopeful.

No doubt I had to trust God more and more and let Him give me the confidence needed.

After nearly two weeks had passed, Barbara and I met Dr. Logi. He appeared to be from the old school, as he was wearing a white shirt and a bowtie, which most doctors do not wear anymore. He explained the surgical procedure and told us that he would remove all the lymph nodes from under my right ear, across my neck and to my Adam's Apple. The area would also extend from the bottom of my jaw to my collarbone. After a long explanation, Dr. Logi referred us to the secretary to set up a time for the surgery and also had her make appointments for a PET Scan, a CT Scan and several other X-rays. I remember distinctly that the appointments were on the day after Easter, Monday, March 31, 1997. From that day forward, I called it "Black Monday."

I cannot tell you about the sermons I preached on that Easter, but you can be assured that the hope of the resurrection was the major topic. Every person has hope because Jesus went to an old, cruel cross and died, was buried and rose the third day. He did this for us. Nothing imaginable I could ever face could be anywhere close to the suffering He took on our behalf. "And he bearing his cross went forth into a place called the place of a skull, which is called in the Hebrew Golgotha: Where they crucified him" (John 19:17-18a).

On Monday, Barbara and I drove to Winston Salem, where all day long the doctors did tests. The first test took place at 7 A.M., and the last took place at 5:30 P.M. Considering the contrast I drank and the injections I received, including Lasix, I kept asking myself, *How will we ever get all this done in one day?* Surprisingly, by 6 P.M. we were through. I prayed all the way through the PET scan, because the Lasix they gave me before the scan seemed to activate my bladder, and twice I had to call the technician to stop and let me go to the restroom. The second time she had to stop the procedure, she warned me that if I had to go again she would have to install a catheter. I surely did not want a catheter, and I did everything I could to complete the scan without another interruption.

Steve and his wife, Leigh Ann, arrived unexpectedly just as Barbara and I were coming out of the MRI building. We went to supper and talked about the long day. Just having them there with us brought peace and comfort to two worn-out souls. The next step would be the surgery.

Another Miracle Coming Up

Yea, though I walk through the valley of the
shadow of death, I will fear no evil:
for thou art with me; thy rod and
thy staff they comfort me.
—Psalm 23:4

FINALLY, THE DAY of the surgery had arrived. Early in the morning, Barbara, Steve and I reported to Baptist Hospital. Steve and Barbara prayed with me, and once again I was rolled off to the operating room. Dr. Logi performed the surgery for about four hours. I can remember the recovery area nurse saying, "Reverend Davis, are you okay?" Of course I responded yes, and then we waited there until I could be taken to my room for overnight observation.

At the beginning, my neck and jaw were sore. The doctor had warned me that one of the dangers of surgery was possibly severing a nerve. Although this did not occur, I did have numbness in the area for a while. Donald and Gail came to the hospital and spent the afternoon with me. Barbara stayed overnight and became my onsite caregiver. I wasn't as much trouble to her this time.

The next morning Dr. Logi came by, examined the wound and bandages, and released me to go home. As usual, we scheduled a follow-up appointment for the next week, and these appointments continued until the healing was complete. In a few weeks I was referred to the oncologist, Dr. Paul Savage, for his examination, and he laid out a plan for continuing my treatment. Later, Dr. Savage and the surgeon would see me on a rotating monthly basis.

My first visit with Dr. Savage was a memorable one. Initially, Barbara and I saw his assistant, and then we met with him for at least an hour. You could say that I was "listening but not listening" when Dr. Savage spoke to us, because I just did not know how to respond. Dr. Savage explained the possibility of the cancer reappearing in some other organs and said that he was prescribing a drug called interferon as a preventive measure to fight the recurrence of the melanoma. He also went though the typical side effects of taking interferon.

Interferon was a drug that had recently been approved for use in the United States. It was generally not available in America during my first occurrence, but the Lord provided a special miracle that made it available to us. If I understood Dr. Savage correctly, the drug was being used on patients who had melanoma for the first time but not with patients who had a recurrence of the disease. However, he was going to try it on me. "For all things come of thee, and of thine own have we given thee" (1 Chron. 29:14b). Miracles can come in the form of drugs! Before leaving, we scheduled an appointment for when I would take my first interferon treatment and be instructed on how to administer it to myself.

I left Dr. Savage's office not really understanding much of what he had said. On the way home, Barbara had to repeat just about everything he had told us. I was about to leap into something that was not inviting and had closed my mind to what I was hearing. Taking shots was not something to which anyone would look forward. The pain in my neck and jaw was aggravating enough without putting something in my body that would probably make me sick.

On May 18, 1997, one week before starting my injections, Ashleigh, Steve and Leigh Ann's daughter, was born. She came really fast—the same afternoon the ladies at the Memorial Baptist Church were giving the couple a baby shower. Leigh Ann began labor at the party and was taken directly to the hospital, where Ashleigh was born within an hour. What a joy it was to have a new baby. It proved that everything in my life was not bad. She would become more than a blessing to me during the next year. "Lo, children are an heritage [blessing] of the Lord: and the fruit of the womb is his reward" (Ps. 127:3a).

When Barbara and I returned to North Carolina Baptist Hospital for the appointment, Dr. Savage answered our questions and then sent us to his nurse for my first injection and training. The nurse gave me the choice of taking the shots in my legs, arms or stomach. The latter two were beyond my comprehension, so I elected to take the shot in my thighs starting just above the knees. This was all new for Barbara and me—neither of us had ever given shots or been responsible for filling vials. The nurse's final recommendation was for me to take the injections at night and to try to keep busy the day after taking them. We knew it was going to be quite a chore. When the nurse had explained everything, she helped me give myself the first injection. Barbara and I left her office somewhat anxious, but we knew that God would again take us through.

Barbara drove home from Winston Salem, and I did not feel any reaction to the injection. When we arrived home, I decided to do what some would call ridiculous and washed all the windows in the house. This kept my mind off the injections and seemed to work for at least the initial day of treatment. Knowing the treatment would have to be administered three nights a week, I pondered the type of activities that I could do in the future to take my mind off taking the interferon. The hospital provided enough medicine to take me through the week.

The next day, I called around to the different pharmacies to determine the best price for interferon. To my surprise, the price of the medicine varied by pharmacy, and the difference was hundreds of dollars. The Winn Dixie Super Market in Kannapolis ultimately became our cheapest supplier. The pharmacy manager agreed to provide the medicine for the next twelve months at the same price.

Before us were twelve months and 156 injections. Everything appeared foggy except for our confidence in a mighty God, Whom we knew would provide our need according to His riches in glory through Christ Jesus our Lord.

Letting God Fight the Daily Battles

Come unto me, all ye that labour and are heavy laden, and I will give you rest. Take my yoke upon you, and learn of me; for I am meek and lowly in heart: and ye shall find rest unto your souls. For my yoke is easy, and my burden is light.
—Matthew 11:28-30

FROM A PHYSICAL and medical standpoint, the worst year of my life had begun. Every week I was going through the tedious steps of filling vials and placing them in the refrigerator, waiting for the day of the week to administer the injection. By far, the job of filling the vials was harder than giving myself the injections. For a person trained in medicine it would have been easy to draw the interferon without getting bubbles in the vial, but for me it was a hard task. Being nervous and having all thumbs did not make the job any easier. But, through God's help, I endured.

I had to administer the medicine every other day. Barbara and I developed a schedule and marked off each day, knowing that it meant one less injection to perform. The injections would be systematically rotated, the first into my left leg and the next into my right. In a short time, the bruises on my legs began to look like a checkerboard. From the first day of the injections, I would place the needle in my upper leg and let Barbara push the plunger to release the contents into my body. I don't know why I had problems releasing the medicine. I guess I trusted her not to hurt me. One of the side effects of the interferon is that it dried out my mouth and caused sores. Barbara and I visited the pharmacy many times to try to get something that might help. I tried candy and chewing gum, but the sores persisted. Medicated chewing gum seemed to work the best, but the taste could have been better. This condition was always worse during the nights and sometimes kept me awake.

Not long after starting the interferon, Dr. Savage instructed me to start seeing a psychologist to help me figure out how to handle the mental part of the treatment. She put me through many exercises that would take my mind off my condition. She also gave me tapes of soothing music that I could use to keep my mind off the treatment.

The appointments were few and the sessions were short, but I felt that what she did was important to the overall treatment process. Cancer not only attacks a person physically but also mentally and spiritually, and these areas must be considered in the treatment.

Though everything was going well, I found myself doing some strange things. One thing that stands out in my mind was that I stopped purchasing clothes. My family gave me some clothes as gifts, but I had no desire to buy them for myself. The only type footwear I would buy were athletic shoes. Also, where in the past I would always keep an ample supply of common toiletries like shaving cream and razor blades on hand, I did not purchase these items unless I had completely run out. Even then, I purchased the smallest size available. In retrospect, I think the reason for this was that down deep, I did not know how much longer I would be around and I did not want them to be wasted. That sounds odd, but cancer patients do not always think like normal people.

I soon started back preaching twice on Sunday. The study and sermon preparation gave me an opportunity to do something other than wait for my next injection. Each day after breakfast, I would lay down on my bed and do my daily devotion. My Bible study was more meaningful during that time than during any other time in my life. The words seemed to come off the page and were immediately stored in my heart. For my edification, I questioned more and searched for answers. "Let the word of Christ dwell in you richly in all wisdom; teaching and admonishing one another in psalms and hymns and spiritual songs, singing with grace in your hearts to the Lord" (Col. 3:16).

Each day the Word became richer and gave me more joy and confidence for what was facing me. Many days I would go downstairs where Barbara was working and tell her what God had said to me through His Word. Though I had been reading through the Bible for a number of years, God seemed to give me a new focus on Bible passages I had somewhat ignored in the past. He kept saying, "Come unto Me, and I will see you through." Surely, peace and comfort was what I was seeking, and God was filling me through His Word as He was healing my body. My loving caregiver, Barbara, was there with me all the way, but the two of us had the mighty hand of God to console us as He revealed His presence and love.

I was getting weaker and wanted to stay in bed more and for longer periods of time. One day, God spoke to my heart and said, "You won't feel as bad if you refuse to give in to this bed and get out and minister to others." That very day, I made the decision to go to the church or visit with church members. When I left our house, Barbara knew that she would see me when I became tired and could go no further. God definitely gave me strength to keep going. When I was trying to help shut-ins or others, my strength seemed to last longer. Without a doubt, God restored my energy and made sure that I had everything I needed to go on. Thank the Lord that even though my body was weakened, I was back doing what He called me to do. "But ye shall receive power, after that the Holy Ghost is come upon you: and ye shall be witnesses unto me both in Jerusalem, and in all Judea, and in Samaria, and unto the uttermost part of the earth" (Acts 1:8).

During the day I could read, watch television and even go and minister to others. It was the nights that were the worst. I slept fairly well, but sometimes I would wake up in the middle of the night and not be able to get back to sleep. Then my mind would start to play tricks on me. Every negative thought that was imaginable would come and try to make me lose my confidence. Thank the Lord that He was available, and within a short time the thoughts that I knew were coming from Satan would diminish. Fortunately, I had learned a number of Bible verses and would keep repeating every one that came to mind. Most of the time, God would give me a peace that put me back to sleep.

While I am in no way suggesting that everyone with cancer can keep on going regardless of how sick he or she may be, God made it work for me. No two people are alike, nor is their cancer treatment the same. I never tell cancer patients how they feel, because the truth is that none of us know how anyone else feels. This is primarily because none of our bodies react the same way to the medicines we are given. Therefore, each of us has to depend upon God and let Him provide what we need for the moment, the day, the week and month. I am glad God spared me and that I can testify to what He did for me.

Helping Others Along the Way

One of His disciples, Andrew, Simon Peter's brother, saith unto him, There is a lad here, which hath five barley loaves, and two small fishes: but what are they among so many? And Jesus said, Make the men sit down. Now there was much grass in the place.

So the men sat down, in number about five thousand. And Jesus took the loaves; and when he had given thanks, he distributed to the disciples, and the disciples to them that were set down; and likewise of the fishes as much as they would. When they were filled, he said to his disciples, Gather up the fragments that remain, that nothing be lost.

—John 6:8-12

WHEN I WAS much younger, I worked with a group of boys at church in an organization called Royal Ambassadors (RA). The program was much like the scouts, but it included a spiritual base for the boys to learn about Jesus Christ. The motto and emphasis of the Royal Ambassadors was "Helping Others in Jesus' Name." As we inducted each child into the Royal Ambassadors, we explained the motto by using the above passage of Scripture where a little boy was willing to give his sack lunch to help Jesus feed 5,000 men. This motto came to mind as I was introduced to a cancer support group. Their goal was to help cancer patients through their ordeal in dealing with cancer.

In the fall of 1997, Barbara and I began to attend a cancer support group offered by the Cabarrus Memorial Hospital (now Carolinas Medical Center-Northeast), which was composed of cancer survivors and their spouses and friends. Although the support group was led by Chaplain Tony Biles and Karen Maxwell, a nurse from the radiation department, there were many helpers of Jesus at each meeting. Both leaders were great at soliciting participation from the attendees and directing the meetings so that the participants had meaningful discussions. Our local American Cancer Society representative, Rachel Watson, also gave the meeting an air of compassion, care and mercy that could only come from one of God's children.

Such meetings typically have all kinds of people in attendance—male and female, old and young, professionals and technicians. None of this mattered, however, for all of us were just survivors with a similar problem trying to make it through the treatments we were taking. Our number one goal was for people to vent their problems, their successes, their needs and their experiences with cancer. From the first meeting, we began to bind together with the objective of helping others in Jesus' name. We also had many local and visiting speakers who gave many insights as to how we could deal with our treatments, including the mental and spiritual aspects.

I talked to Dr. Savage, my oncologist, about the importance of support groups. He highly recommended such groups, as he believed that cancer patients could learn more about how to handle their cancer from each other than from the doctors. He said, "The doctor provides the medication for the treatment, but living with the disease and the effects that different medicines have on patients can only come from those who are experiencing it." Although those in the support group were different individuals with bodies and minds that reacted differently to medications, there were many commonalities that we could share.

Each month, nausea seemed to be one of the main topics. The attendees learned from each other about the types of medicines used to treat nausea. In some cases, the cancer survivors learned about available medicines and discussed these with their doctors. Sure enough, the new medications worked or were at least partially effective in treating their symptoms.

In the beginning, I felt somewhat alone because I was the only person attending the group who was suffering from melanoma. No one was available for me to talk about my disease. Sometimes I wondered if anyone had ever survived melanoma. But thank the Lord, just a few meetings later a man with melanoma who had previously been with the group showed up. He had moved to Virginia, but he was back in the area for a while. What a wonderful assurance it was to know that he had gone through the treatment and had now been cancer-free for more than ten years. Any cancer survivor eagerly seeks good news, and this man's testimony was certainly a lift for me.

Another bit of advice I received from the support group was how to handle the anxiety that always accompanied doctor follow-ups. I had previously dealt with this issue somewhat, but I did not know if what I was experiencing was normal. The group confirmed that when an upcoming doctor's appointment was near, the anxieties would begin to build. Though the feelings were not necessarily fear, the thought of being told that you were doing something wrong or that the treatment was not working or that the cancer had somehow spread was not welcome news. The unknown brings a feeling of despair that cannot be described. It's impossible to describe the emptiness you feel until you hear the words, "All is okay." The relief those words bring is like a ton of weight being lifted from your chest.

The support group always agreed to have prayer, and these prayers were not politically correct or directed to some "higher power." We prayed to Almighty God, Who sent His only begotten Son to earth to give us eternal life as well as a full and meaningful life in Him. Prayer was a vital resource for me in making it through the treatments and defeating the disease that I was currently battling.

Our closing prayer was always a highlight of the meeting. The group selected members with special needs and invited them into the middle of the circle. The rest of us would then cross our bodies with our arms and take the hand of the person on our right and our left. As we encircled those in the middle, we got closer and closer until we could just about embrace them. Then Chaplain Biles or one of the members would offer a prayer asking God to give those in the middle of the circle a portion of His loving care. He would also pray that God would sustain all those who were present and those in the group who could not attend that night. We left the meeting knowing God would see us through whatever obstacles that tried to beset us and with a feeling of unity in knowing we did not walk alone.

During the initial treatments, God provided others to lend support to me. One such person was Dr. Dewey Hobbs, who spent many years in service at the Baptist State Convention of North Carolina and the North Carolina Baptist Hospital. I learned through Dr. Randy Wadford of the Cabarrus Baptist Association that Dewey had gone through a bout with melanoma and was doing very well. I didn't know how many years he had survived at the time, but for me his story provided a light at the end of the tunnel. During one of my appointments with Dr. Savage, Dewey met me at the Baptist Hospital Oncology Department. Dewey shared his experience with me and was very encouraging. He also told me how his doctor at Duke Medical Center had recommended that he take vitamins, which I still do to this day.

Another encourager was Betty Fulton, the wife of Bill Fulton, a co-worker at Fieldcrest Cannon Industries. Prior to my being diagnosed with cancer, Betty had battled breast cancer, and I had visited her in the hospital. She always had such a positive attitude. By the time of my detection she was far into her treatment. I can remember her telling me about the chemo and the side effects. One thing she told me that I will always remember is about how after her treatments were completed the thought of recurrence still loomed in the back of her mind. She said that even when she got a toothache, she would question if it was being caused by the cancer.

Betty was a real jewel in showing me how a positive attitude could go a long way in getting me through the days that followed. Betty trusted her God in much the same way that King David described in Psalm 37:3-5: "Trust in the LORD, and do good; so shalt thou dwell in the land, and verily thou shalt be fed. Delight thyself also in the LORD; and he shall give thee the desires of thine heart. Commit thy way unto the LORD; trust also in him; and he shall bring it to pass."

A Major Setback

*And He said unto me, My grace is sufficient
for thee: for my strength is made perfect in
weakness. Most gladly therefore will I rather
glory in my infirmities, that the power of
Christ may rest upon me.*
—2 Corinthians 12:9

EVERYTHING WAS GOING well. I was back at work fulfilling all my duties in the church and feeling fairly good considering the fact that the side effects of the interferon still left me drained. I don't remember much about my daily activities, but I recall that the church was in the middle of a building program. We sold bonds to raise enough money to build a family life center, expand our Sunday school space and remodel the front foyer of the church auditorium. Much was being accomplished by the Lord, but I had a problem understanding why I couldn't be involved in the task the members had committed to do in the construction.

As 1998 approached, Barbara and I were looking forward to getting the interferon behind us. The five remaining months were much closer than the seven already behind us. Nevertheless, on the last Friday night of January, Barbara and I were at home enjoying television when I began to have pain in my chest like I had never before experienced. Though I had had a little chest pain that morning, it was nothing like what I was experiencing at this time. The pain was in the center of my chest and not in my arms, jaw or neck. The impact was almost more than I could withstand.

Because I had been eating popcorn, I concluded that it was just a bad case of heartburn. At the time I couldn't remember ever previously having heartburn, so I had very little with which to make a comparison. I immediately began to walk around the house because the pain would not let me sit. This must have gone on for twenty to thirty minutes before it stopped. Not knowing much about chest pain other than the fact that it was serious, I stuck with my conclusion that it must have been heartburn caused by the popcorn and a chocolate sweet I had eaten.

On Saturday I did not feel great, but I continued with my plans to preach on Sunday. The next day when I went to church I was feeling weak, but I thought it would go away. I struggled when I spoke that morning, but I finished the message. I sat down as soon as I could and asked the youth pastor, Tim Gold, to close the service.

When the service concluded, Barbara pleaded with me to go to the emergency room for an exam, but, being hardheaded, I said no. She gave me an ultimatum: If I didn't agree to go right then, I would see our family physician, Dr. George Monroe, the next day. I agreed to the latter.

The next day, I made an appointment with Dr. Monroe for the afternoon. He ordered an electro-cardiogram. As you can guess, the report revealed that I had had a heart attack. The doctor indicated that the attack had been light but that it was still serious. I drove myself to the emergency room at the Northeast Medical Center to be admitted. On the way there, I called Barbara to give her the bad news. Of course, she came to the emergency room as fast as she could.

When she arrived, she accompanied me from the emergency unit to the heart monitoring unit. Once there, Doctor Paul Campbell examined me and said that I would need a heart catheterization, which would probably be done the next day. Waiting was nothing new for me. That afternoon I had many visitors, including my children. Most people offered a prayer for me before leaving. "The effectual fervent prayer of a righteous man availeth much" (Jas. 5:16b).

As usual, Barbara stayed with me through the night. Per routine, I had nothing to eat or drink except my medicine for the morning. The procedure was scheduled for 11 A.M. Barbara, Gail, Steve and I waited until finally, about noon, the attendant came to get me. Steve prayed for me, and then the family and I were taken to the heart catheterization lab. My experience as a pastor had always been to be the one on the outside waiting, but never as the patient. I would finally learn what a heart catheterization was all about.

The technician placed the tube into my groin and gave me all the precautions about not pulling it out, as it was inserted in an artery. Dr. David Beard, a cardiologist, performed the actual catheterization procedure. He talked all the way through the procedure and showed me on a screen the blockages in the lower part of my heart. One vessel was 95 percent blocked and the other was 75 percent blocked. Dr. Beard also indicated that I was not a candidate for angioplasty because of where the blockage was located. Nevertheless, he thought that I was a good candidate for heart bypass surgery, but he said that he would need to consult with the other doctors. He left the room, and I waited.

Dr. Beard returned in a short time and said that after consulting with the other doctors, he believed the best treatment was with medicine, a beta-blocker. The only reason he gave was that if I had bypass surgery, I would have to come off the interferon because it impeded healing. However, he said that if the medication did not prove effective, they would consider surgery at a later date. As I waited to return to my room, I thanked God that He had spared me and asked that I would never have to face bypass surgery. "O give thanks unto the LORD, for He is good: for his mercy endureth forever" (Ps. 136:1).

My doctors instructed that I had to lie completely still with my leg perfectly straight for the next six hours. I was hungry, so the nurse brought me a plate with some type of stew and rice. Since I could not move, Steve fed it to me. As I was eating, my stomach began to hurt badly, and the pain this caused in addition to the pain of having to stay on my back without moving made me more than irritable.

The nurse who came in for the night shift was a real "doozy," as Hazel used to say on an old television series. The nurse had absolutely no compassion and let me lie on my back for thirty minutes longer than the normal six hours before getting me up. When she finally took the time to get me up, she rushed letting me sit up on the side of the bed and my blood pressure and pulse dropped to dangerously low levels. I immediately felt terrible. She ran Barbara out of the room and called for assistance. She gave me some type of injection and moved the bed in such a way that I was almost standing on my head. In a short time my blood pressure was back under control. I never wanted to see that lady again, no matter what happened. I was an unhappy camper for the rest of the night and felt very bad. My stomach continued to ache even after I took an antacid medicine.

The next day my brother, John, my sisters, Miriam, Magilee and Shirley, my children and many from the church came to visit me. In the afternoon, Dr. Beard ran some type of treadmill test and determined that I was doing well. At this point, the truth was that my stomach was giving me more problems than my heart. We stayed another night, but I told the nurse in charge of the unit that I would go home if I was given the same nurse as before. Thank the Lord she was off that night.

The next morning I was discharged from the hospital. Unfortunately, I had the worst case of diarrhea in my life. Nothing seemed to help. I did not want to eat anything—not even chicken noodle soup, which had always been my favorite to help me get over any type of stomach problems. In the days to come, I had problems getting used to the correct dosage of the beta-blocker, which made me feel dizzy. This only complicated my stomach problem, which was steadily getting worse.

Within a few days, we made an appointment with Dr. Monroe. He did a stool sample and discovered that while I was in the hospital I had contracted clostridium difficile, a bacterial infection of the intestine. This condition had weakened me as much or more than the heart attack. Another problem that I did not need had been placed on me. However, God gave me even more strength to overcome it. "But we have this treasure in earthen vessels, that the excellency of the power may be of God, and not of us" (2 Cor. 4:7).

A Double Dose of Recovery

*It is of the Lord's mercies that we are not
consumed, because His compassions fail not.*
—Lamentations 3:22

IN FEBRUARY 1998, I attended the orientation for cardiac rehab. I really did not know the toll that the interferon, the heart attack and the intestinal infection had had on my body until I started the cardiac rehab regimen. Never in my life had I had trouble doing any type of physical exercise, but quickly I found that I had to reach way back for energy to keep going.

The rehab program addressed aspects of the patient's physical, mental, spiritual and dietary health. Treatment in all these areas was necessary to move the patient toward recovery. I can not say enough about the excellent care and compassion I received from the staff at the Northeast Medical Center Health and Fitness Center. The team consisted of Susan Herring, an exercise physicist, and nurses Kim Olsson, Vicky Farthing and Carla Smith, who spent every moment of each session moving the applicants toward their goal to recovery. I did not even have to be around Mike Shinn, the manager of this unit, to be convinced that the team and Mike had one objective: to get their patients well. "I will lift up mine eyes unto the hills, from whence cometh my help. My help cometh from the LORD, which made heaven and earth" (Ps.121:1-2).

I was only in the rehab program for a few weeks when I experienced some light chest pains. Dr. Monroe diagnosed it as a pulled muscle. This set me back for a day or two, because the nurse did not think I should continue with the full program. New people were coming into the cardiac rehab program every week, and others were graduating, having finished the twelve weeks. The work was hard, but we still had time to establish relationships with the other participants. As in the cancer support group, we were able to talk and learn from each other. The members who were further along often gave encouragement to those who were new in the program. Talking to each other was not a matter of "misery loving company" but genuine support to help each other along the way.

Not really understanding how much fluid a body needed, I became very ill one morning and had to go to the emergency room at Northeast Medical Center. Naturally, this caused another delay for a couple of days as I was treated in the hospital for dehydration. I have since learned that drinking liquids is absolutely necessary to keep a body healthy. This is even more important when the body has undergone a setback such as mine.

The cardiac rehab continued, and I kept my checkups with Dr. Leshin and Dr. Savage. I could not have asked for better care than they gave to me. Both instructed me to do self-exams at least one a week. They also examined me periodically for any possible skin irregularities, and performed yearly chest X-rays and blood work. Without hesitation, I would say that I am alive today because of these two men. They did not take melanoma lightly, and they were always available to see me on short notice to check on any possible abnormality that was causing me concern.

I cannot remember the month or date, but in the spring of 1998 I experienced chest pain and ended up in the hospital for another night. Neither the emergency room doctor nor the cardiologist could give me any explanation for the pain, though it might have been caused by a gallbladder attack. Sometime later, I had to have my gallbladder removed. Nonetheless, I was so thankful that it was not my heart, because if that had been the case, I am sure I would have had to have bypass surgery.

That evening, many people came to the emergency room and prayed for me while I was being examined. "Be careful [anxious] for nothing; but in every thing by prayer and supplication with thanksgiving let your requests be made known unto God" (Phil. 4:6).

C h a p t e r   1 0

Recognizing
a Victory

But thanks be to God, which giveth us the
victory through our Lord Jesus Christ.
—1 Corinthians 15:57

IF I HAD to do it all over again, I would have maintained a journal of my experiences with melanoma. Because I didn't keep a daily journal, in most cases I cannot remember the exact dates when something occurred; but one thing I know for certain is that my last interferon injection was on May 18, 1998. The reason I remember this date is because my granddaughter, Ashleigh, had been born one year earlier, the week the shots began.

Barbara and I had gone to Williamsburg, Virginia, with our friends David and Pinkie Archer, and I had had one more injection, number 156, that week.

We had a wonderful time in Virginia, but nothing made me happier than to finish the interferon. We went out to dinner that night to celebrate. This was shouting time. No more preparing vials or having to remember which leg had been given the shot the last time or figuring out where to place the injection. Thank the Lord it was all over.

My physical condition did not change at that very moment, but my mental and spiritual demeanor was elevated higher than anyone can imagine. I did not know how long it would take for my physical strength to be restored, but I was happy. My mind went back to twelve months earlier when the treatment seemed like an insurmountable task. Though I may have taken that view, my God knew that He would see me through. Thank God that He knows the future and already knew I would overcome. "O taste and see that the LORD is good: blessed is the man that trusteth in Him" (Ps. 34:8).

A milestone had been completed and I had a glimpse of light at the end of the tunnel, but the journey was far from over. I know from the cancer support group members that the disease has a way of recurring, so my hope is in the Lord and Him alone. Psalm 23 tells me that He will take me through the shadow of death. He has prepared a table before me in the presence of my enemies, and my cup runs over. Surely God's goodness and mercy will follow me all the days of my life. He is present and will see me through whatever trials I may have to face in the future.

Post Treatment: Almost Twelve Years Later

*What shall we then say to these things? If
God be for us, who can be against us? Nay, in
all these things we are more than conquerors
through Him that loved us.*
—Romans 8:31,37

SEVENTEEN YEARS HAVE passed since I was
diagnosed with melanoma, and God has blessed
me in that I have not had a recurrence. As a cancer
survivor I know that I cannot lower my guard, because the disease has the possibility of coming back
at any time. Yet I do not live in fear. During these
eleven-plus years, since completing the interferon
treatment, I have returned to Dr. Leshin to have him
check spots or nodes that were suspicious. On each
occasion, I prayed, "Lord, I don't want it again, but

You know what is best. You have brought me this far, and if it should be back, I can deal with it as long as I have You."

During one of my check-ups, I identified a raised place on my leg for Dr. Leshin to examine. He immediately said that it was basal cell carcinoma, another type of skin cancer. He told me that he could take care of it with no problem, and he did.

I have also made many trips between Concord, North Carolina, and Winston Salem, North Carolina, where my two cancer doctors are located. My check-ups began at six-month intervals, but were eventually extended to twelve months. However, I still see Dr. Leshin, my dermatologist, and Dr. Savage, my oncologist, on a six-month basis. Dr. Leshin does the physical skin scan, while Dr. Savage performs a chest X-ray and does a blood review. These two doctors and my Lord have kept me free of melanoma for all these years. I am thankful that God gave me two compassionate professionals who give me topnotch care.

Memorial Baptist Church finished the new addition of a family life center, extension of the church auditorium and additional Sunday school rooms. A dedication service was held on June 7, 1998. The church leaders laid twelve stones at the front of the church to commemorate how God had blessed the church and brought her through the building expansion. This was similar to what the Israelites did when they crossed over the Jordan River to enter into the Promised Land. The twelve stones representing the twelve tribes of Israel were taken from the middle of the river and placed on the other side as a monument signifying that God had brought them through safely. Our objective as a church was for later generations to see these stones and remember God's blessings.

In September 1999, Barbara and I were invited to go to South Africa on a mission trip. Although I had not yet regained my full strength, we joined the team along with Amy and Ronnie Raper, a young couple from Memorial Baptist Church. When we arrived in Johannesburg, South Africa, we immediately left for Port Shepstone, a city located on the Indian Ocean.

Our sponsor for the trip was Port Shepstone Baptist Church. The church had a young pastor, Darryl Soal, and he and his wife, Marianne, had done a great job in planning a multi-church preaching crusade that was being held in a large tent. Darryl had brought churches of all denominations together, and there were speaking engagements at different locations every morning, afternoon and evening. The four of us had to hit the road preaching and speaking at many different types of venues, including jails, businesses, social clubs and schools. I quickly discovered that this would be the first real challenge to test my physical stamina. Thank God, He provided what I needed to meet the task. We were able to finish at Port Shepstone, visit a game park and hold revival services at another church.

Although I was progressively getting better, my energy was not coming back as quickly as I expected. With the new construction completed, Memorial Baptist Church needed to reach out to the community. Our members had made a great commitment to reach people for the Lord, but unfortunately I did not know how long it would take me to be able to effectively lead them. It was the hardest decision I ever made, but on the spur of the moment I announced to the church that I would retire on January 1, 2000—one-and-a-half years after my treatment was completed. The church needed a pastor with much more energy than I could give at the time.

I walked away and never looked back. For years, my advice to people who had worked for me had been that if you make the decision to leave a position, don't look back or regret what you had done. If God is leading a person to new employment, whether in a secular job or in the ministry, He will provide. In my case, I left the congregation of Memorial Baptist Church, some of the most precious people in the world, knowing it was God's will. I knew that if I stepped aside, our Lord would use the next pastor in moving the church forward to do what He had planned for that body of believers.

After leaving Memorial Baptist Church, God allowed me to regain my strength and become an interim pastor at the First Baptist Church of Enochville in Kannapolis, North Carolina. The people at Enochville welcomed Barbara and me and treated us as if we were there full-time. We enjoyed their fellowship for the year we served them as much as anything we have done in the ministry. If God had been calling me back to full-time service, I would loved to have stayed there longer. The new pastor was called to that church, and he is doing well there.

Immediately after leaving Enochville Baptist, Barbara and I were asked to work with a new church plant at Friendship Southern Baptist Church in Concord, North Carolina. During that time, the leadership led the church into buying property and constructing a new building. They were a wonderful group of people, but God did not lead us to go there permanently. Again, our stay was for just a year.

God next led us to Shadybrook Baptist Church in Kannapolis, North Carolina. This time, God let us serve that congregation for three exciting years. The duration of our stay there was twice as long as that of the previous pastor, and we knew our Lord had selected us to remain longer with that congregation. They, too, were special, and we came to love and respect them. When our task was completed, God already had another pastor ready to take the reins and move the people forward.

Just recently, Barbara and I completed a six-month stay at Odell Baptist Church in Concord, North Carolina, as their supply pastor. Our time there was short, but the blessing was ours as we got to know another group of God's people.

In addition to being given the opportunity to serve God in churches, He has allowed Barbara and me to travel to Europe, Great Britain, India and South Africa. We have been on mission trips to South

Africa thirteen times and have traveled to places in Romania, Scotland and India. A special joy for us has been to take our daughter, Gail, her son, Josh, and our granddaughter Brittany on mission adventures in South Africa and Romania. We have also traveled to the Big Island of Hawaii with our family to assist a church in their Vacation Bible School. I absolutely believe that God has spared me not only to serve churches but also to take the Word of God overseas to people who have never heard the news that Jesus saves. Twelve years ago, I would have never thought any of this would have been possible.

Barbara and I have remained busy doing many things, including follow-up appointments with Dr. Leshin and Dr. Savage. They have done everything possible to prevent the recurrence of my melanoma. These appointments no longer create the anxiety in me that they did at one time. Yes, I love to hear both of them say that everything looks good, but I don't have that knot in my stomach that I used to have during follow-up appointments. I am confident that I am in God's hands and that no matter what happens, He has promised to never leave me or forsake me. He is my peace. "And the peace of God, which passeth all understanding, shall keep your hearts and minds through Christ Jesus" (Phil. 4:7).

An Ounce of Prevention

*For to one is given by the Spirit the word of
wisdom; to another the word of knowledge
by the same Spirit.*
—1 Corinthians 12:8

YOU CAN READILY recognize the title of this chapter from the saying, "An ounce of prevention is worth a pound of cure." In the following section, I provide a list of "do's" and "don'ts" to help cancer patients deal with their condition. Note that not all of these preventative measures apply to every cancer patient, so these should be taken for what they are worth. These are just some things that I have learned that helped me through my treatment and survival (which continues today). I do not profess to know all the answers; I just want to pass these tips on to those who can use them. "Strengthen ye the weak hands, and confirm the feeble knees" (Isa. 35:3).

1. If you do not know the Lord Jesus Christ as your Savior, ask Him for forgiveness of your sins and accept Him as your Lord and Savior. Do not hesitate one moment; turn away from your sins and turn to Jesus. Simply pray, "Lord Jesus, I need You and want You to be my Savior. I am hereby asking You to forgive my sins and save me. I believe You are the Son of God Who died on the cross, was buried and rose on the third day for me. Lord Jesus, come into my heart right now and take control of my life. Save me! I commit my life to You."

    You don't have to say these exact same words, but pray something similar. The important thing is that you ask forgiveness, confess Jesus as Lord and ask Him to come into your heart. Having Jesus on your side will make it much easier to make it through what you are facing. "For whosoever shall call upon the name of the Lord shall be saved" (Rom. 10:13).

2. If you think you might have symptoms that could be related to cancer, go to a doctor immediately. In the case of skin concerns, have a doctor check out any abnormal skin conditions or moles that have changed form or color. I wish that I had gone to a

dermatologist much sooner than I did. My condition was treatable, but if I had waited longer it could have been fatal. "Happy is the man that findeth wisdom, and the man that getteth understanding" (Prov. 3:13).

3. Listen to your doctors and follow their instructions. Pray that God will provide doctors whom you can trust to do what is best for you. If you feel that you are not getting the treatment you need, you can always ask to be referred to another doctor for a second opinion. Again, I feel strongly that God will give you the wisdom to know when you need to go elsewhere for help. "Casting all your care upon him; for he careth for you" (1 Pet. 5:7).

4. Ask your doctor about any medicines you have heard about that are helping other people with a similar condition. My support group was constantly sharing information about the different medicines they were using for a condition. Remember that your doctor is the professional and has the last say, but I feel confident that doctors want to do what is best for their patients.

5. Be careful not to try to be the doctor. When comparing your symptoms to those of others, remember that two people with the same type of cancer might have to be treated differently because of certain extenuating

circumstances. Again, you must trust the doctors to do what is right.

6. Researching statistical data that relates to your type of cancer and condition is not always in your best interest. These statistics can be very depressing. When I was diagnosed with melanoma a second time, I went on the Internet to research my condition and prognosis. I came away from my computer feeling really down, because the prognosis was not good. I was not looking for a rosy picture, but when I read that I had a 30 percent chance of survival within five years, my heart hit the floor.

    When I asked one doctor about the statistic, he gave me some great advice: "You are not a statistic but one of God's children. He loves you and is going to care for you as His own. Forget the statistics and trust God for your survival." The doctor was right: we are God's creation, and He handles each of us individually. "I will praise thee; for I am fearfully and wonderfully made: marvelous are thy works; and that my soul knoweth right well" (Ps. 139:14).

7. Keep a positive attitude if possible. One of the toughest things to do during treatment is remain positive, especially when the medicines you are taking work the opposite as expected and you just don't feel good. Yet studies show that those who have a

positive outlook heal faster and do not have as many complications. During my cancer and heart treatments, I was taught that whenever possible I should keep my head up high and look to the bright side. Having a strong relationship with the Lord will also help, because I know that if I offload my burdens and give them to our Lord, He has promised to carry them for me. Never give up, no matter how grave the situation may be. My brother-in-law, Gene Thompson, who was very sick for years and spent many days in the hospital, would often say, "I may get down, but I will never give up." We must keep faith in our God. "Now faith is the substance of things hoped for, the evidence of things not seen" (Heb. 11:1).

8. Join a cancer support group if possible. The oncology department at your local hospital will typically know when and where these groups meet. I have already provided an explanation of the benefits of cancer support groups in this book; if you give these groups a chance, I am confident that you will like what you find. The Bible tells us to help others, for it is better to give than to receive (see Acts 20:35).

9. Continue to exercise, if you are physically able to do so. Experience has shown that physical exercise will help your body fight the cancer. One time in the cardiac rehab

program, our guest speaker shared some statistics on how exercising improves a person's chance of survival, no matter what type of medical condition that person may have. I started a regular workout routine in cardiac rehab and have continued it to this day. Even when I am feeling bad, I still try to do some type of physical exercise, and I normally go away feeling better.

10. Pray and ask others to pray for you. Prayer is important in getting through the devastating days of cancer treatment. God told the prophet Jeremiah, "Call unto me, and I will answer thee, and shew thee great and mighty things, which thou knowest not" (Jer. 33:3). God calls us to pray and promises that He will provide the answers that are beyond our imagination. I can't think of a better time to pray than when you are fighting a battle with a terrible disease. Also, you need the prayers of others. I know the prayers that were offered to God on my behalf were one of the most important factors in my recovery.

11. Do not ignore your caregiver, the one beside you every day who gives you support and the special love you need. Yes, as a cancer patient you endure awful treatment day in and day out, but the caregiver is right there holding your hand, praying and taking loads of stress that are not identifiable to the naked eye.

This stress can build up, which is why these special loved ones need time to get away, rest their bodies for a while and let the pressure and anxieties go. Do not let your caregiver become sick because of overwork and strain. Let them know that it is okay for them to get away for a while.

12. Recognize that you are not living a dream and that everything that is happening to you is real. You have to face the good and the bad. Reports from the doctors will differ, but you have to go on believing that God will get you through and that truly "this too will pass." God never promised us a rose garden, but He will be with us in both the sunshine and the rain. At times you may have to pinch yourself, but know that what you are experiencing is real and that God will see you through.

13. Stay out of direct sunlight when you can. My dermatologist told me that my problem started because of over-exposure to the sun. In my youth I was just like all the rest and wanted a tan. If I had known what it was doing to me, I would have taken preventative measures, as I do today. No matter who you are or the type of skin you have, the rule is to have on a strong sunblock when out in sunlight. Also, as much as possible, cover your arms and your head. No one wants to hear a doctor say, "I am sorry, but you have

melanoma." In addition, help your children protect their skin. Heredity plays a part in people being inflicted with melanoma.

I hope these recommendations will help you through your treatment. Remember that these are not coming from a doctor but from someone who has been there and wants to help you.

What Does the Future Bring?

Jesus Christ the same yesterday,
and today, and forever.
—Hebrews 13:8

I WISH I knew what tomorrow will bring, but I can be sure that God holds the future and that I can only continue to trust Him. He has brought me this far, and I have no reason to believe that He won't continue to take me through every obstacle, no matter how large it may be. As every cancer survivor knows, I am just a survivor—nothing more and nothing less. Jesus promised His disciples when He went away that He would give them a Comforter, the Holy Spirit. Those who know the Holy Spirit know that He is always with them and is ever close to be their helper. He is the type of helper who will hold their hands and take them through whatever situation they have to face. "So that we may boldly say, the Lord is my helper" (Heb. 13:6a).

One of my goals is to try to help others deal with their situations. Survivors have an upper hand in encouraging others through their walk with cancer, because we have been there and can give advice on something that may be bothering that person at the time. My experience was only with one type of chemotherapy (interferon), but I have spent time in the waiting room of the radiation lab, holding patients' hands and praying for their recovery. Having been where they are walking makes consoling chemo patients much easier. As I already mentioned, I never try to give the impression that I know exactly what they are experiencing, but I can still talk with them and give them any advice that proved true for me. All God wants is for us to make ourselves available. None of us are excellent counselors. We are witnesses as to what we have gone through.

I pray this little book has been a help to you. If so, pass a copy on to another person to help them through their cancer experience.

The Real Survivors

But he that doeth truth cometh to the light,
that his deeds may be made manifest, that
they are wrought in God.
—John 3:21

I COULD NOT close this book without addressing the "real survivors." A number of years ago, one of the television networks began producing a show called *Survivor,* in which the contestants are placed under unfamiliar conditions and circumstances in a desolate place. The person who lasts the longest wins a monetary prize and is designated "the sole survivor." The program is still very popular, but it has never truly identified the real survivors of this world.

I think of a survivor as one who has gone through a life-or-death ordeal. In the 1970s, Zalin Grant, my wife's cousin, wrote a book called *The Survivors*, which was about survivors of the Vietnam War. The characters were real survivors. Thousands of the veterans walked away from combat with their bodies mutilated and with minds that even today cannot escape the horrible battles they fought and endured. These veterans may have escaped the war, but for many of them the fighting continues on today. These men and women are not playing a game but are true survivors and heroes.

Another group of true survivors are those who have survived the dreadful disease called cancer. Though I have not experienced being in actual combat as those who have fought in wars, I know something about being a cancer survivor. I am still living through it and have many friends who are experiencing the same.

Cancer inflicts the body and the mind, similar to hand-to-hand combat. Whether you are currently being treated or the disease is in remission, it never leaves you completely. You have to constantly deal with the question of when it will reappear and when the fighting will begin all over again. The battle that takes place in the mind is a close second to the battle that takes place during the physical treatment. There are good days and bad days. Even on the good days, you will never be able to completely erase the thought that the cancer may still be within you or that it may recur. The smallest pain of any kind can set off the panic button—and then the thing you want to forget the most is suddenly back upon you.

Yes, survivors of cancer learn to cope with the disease using whatever methods best suit them. Most of the survivors I know learn to turn it over to what some have called a "higher power." We Christians know Him as Jesus, Who loves us and gave His life for us. He has given us His Word to give us confidence to go on. "There is no fear in love; but perfect love casteth out fear: for fear hath torment. He that feareth is not perfect love" (1 John 4:18).

The Bible has many encouraging passages that can help a child of God in his or her struggle with the ills of cancer. We do not know what tomorrow brings, but we do know that it is God who brings tomorrow. Jesus Christ has given us the invitation to place our burdens on Him. He promises rest unto our souls. The true survivors of cancer or any other dreadful disease can find refuge in God and God alone. Remember the words of the psalmist and take comfort: "God is our refuge and strength, a very present help in trouble" (Ps. 46:1).

So when people talk about survivors, make sure you make it clear that true survivors are fighting for their lives. They could be here today and gone tomorrow.

PW